THE

NEW YORK

Steam Cable Towing Company.

THE BELGIAN SYSTEM OF CABLE TOWING

AS RELATING TO THE USE OF

STEAM ON THE CANALS

AND THE QUESTION OF CHEAP TRANSPORTATION.

Office:
NO. 40 BROADWAY, NEW YORK.
Room 26.

ALBANY:
WEED, PARSONS AND COMPANY, PRINTERS.
1875.

GOV. CLINTON.

[The cut on the opposite page is a representation of the tow-boats employed by this company in towing canal boats by means of a submerged cable and clip-drum.]

The system is simple, consisting of a wire cable laid on the bottom of the canal through its entire length, and fastened at the two extreme ends; and a steam tow-boat, provided with an additional engine, to which is attached a clip-drum, or grooved driving wheel, with suitable guiding and tightening pulleys. Thus equipped, and the boats to be towed made fast to the tow-boat, the process of towing is performed by lifting the cable from the bottom of the canal by means of a grapple, and placing it over the clip-drum. This drum is then put in motion (turned) by machinery in the tow-boat, causing the cable to pass over it without slipping, and fall back again into the canal at the stern of the tow-boat. Thus the tow-boat is drawn along the cable, and consequently through the canal, with the same facility that a locomotive is drawn on the rails, with this difference: the rail is stationary and the locomotive *wheel passes over it*, while the *cable* is flexible and *passes over the drum*. The tow-boats used, and the boats towed thereby, can be passed through the locks with the same facility as those towed by animal power. The immense commerce of the Erie canal will require two cables—one for the *up* and another for the *down* boats.

Although the article contained in this pamphlet was published two years ago, there is only a little change to be made in regard to details of operation, so as to include the whole season of 1876, in now using it as a reliable and conservative statement of the great benefits to the State and City of New York, and all interests connected with or relating to the Canal, resulting from the general introduction and use of the Belgian system.

It is very gratifying to those interested in the application of the Belgian system to the Erie Canal since the year 1871, that all merits heretofore claimed and estimates of profits to be made, have been confirmed as near as is possible, by the results of practical operations on a very limited scale.

EMERSON FOOTE.

New York, Feb. 1877.

THE BELGIAN SYSTEM OF CABLE TOWING

AS RELATING TO THE USE OF STEAM ON THE CANALS AND THE QUESTION OF CHEAP TRANSPORTATION.

The Belgian system of towing on rivers or canals by a steam-tug, working on a submerged chain or wire rope, has been in profitable operation on European rivers and canals for many years. The men who had successfully operated this system in Europe, visited this country, to introduce it on the great inland rivers and canals, but were unsuccessful, principally on account of their large demands for patent rights. In the year 1869, some Americans, who were very favorably impressed with their knowledge of the system, raised sufficient money to defray the expense of sending an agent to Belgium, to examine and test the working of the system and to introduce it upon the Erie canal, under a State charter, granting exclusive rights to use this system upon the canals of the State of New York. Their agent, being perfectly satisfied with his inspection and with the personal working of this system in Europe, purchased at Liege duplicate machinery of that he had operated, and, upon his return, constructed a boat after plans obtained from Belgium to contain it. Six miles of steel wire rope completed the required equipment, and, having been submerged on the canal from the Albany basin, through the locks, to Troy, the steam tug "Gov. Clinton" was most successfully worked upon the cable, and thus for the first time the Belgian system was introduced upon the Erie canal. This was in the year 1871.

The New York Steam Cable Towing Company was organized on the 1st day of November, 1871, to operate this system of steam towage upon the canals of this State, and, in an act to confer additional powers upon the company, passed March 8th, 1872, the State recognized the company as duly organized in conformity with the provisions of the law.

The company built that year another steam cable tower called the "M. M. Caleb," and, having purchased 26 miles more of steel wire rope, were enabled to equip the 31 miles of the Erie canal between Buffalo and Lockport with a single line of cable, and work thereon the two steam cable towers the company now owned. This portion of the canal was the most disadvantageous for the working of the Belgian system that can be found in the State. It was very crooked, included Tonawanda creek, which is full of sunken trees and rafts, and with an eastward current, between Buffalo and Black Rock, of from two to four miles the hour. This level was purposely selected to test the system under the greatest difficulties. From the season of canal navigation of the year 1871 up to that just closed of 1874, the Belgian system has been worked, for a whole or part of each season, in a perfectly satisfactory manner. No practical or mechanical difficulties now exist; it has the good will and patronage of the canal boatmen, and has never failed, after rigid investigation, to receive the indorsement of the many eminent men acquainted with the wants of the canal, or possessed of the best engineering, mechanical or financial abilities.

The following results have been obtained: Nine canal boats, or 1400 tons of freight, have been taken in one tow against the current at Black Rock. In all operations no limit of power has been developed. Machinery can be bought in England guaranteed to take 2000 tons of freight four miles the hour. A speed of three miles the hour is readily obtained, but all special tests at Buffalo have shown from four and one-half to six miles the hour, with 1000 tons of freight in tow, going against current. The expense of a cable tow-boat will not exceed $30 for 24 hours. In 37 days 38 tons of coal were consumed. The tow-boat will cost about $10,000. Last season the "M. M. Caleb" ran continuously 792 miles between Tonawanda and Buffalo, without an accident or delay of any kind, and no repairs of machinery or boat. An iron wire cable costs $1,000 per mile, and at Cologne, where a ferry has for many years used this system, a one and one-eighth inch cable stands 15,000 passages. The daily expenses of the "M. M. Caleb," capable of towing 2500 tons of freight, are no more than the best steam self-propelling canal boat, carrying 200 tons of freight.

Canal boats towed by a cable towing boat four miles the hour, displace less water than when towed by animal power one and one-half miles the hour.

There is no wash to banks in cable towing, the only disturbance to the water being a wire rope, raised from the surface about twenty feet in advance of the boat, and the passage of the boat through the water.

Curves are easily rounded. The slack of the cable is readily managed. There are no kinks or breakages by use. The wire cable is spliced as readily as a hemp rope. The time in locking amounts to little as compared with the time saved by increased speed. For instance, it requires 65 hours to go by animal power from Rochester to Buffalo, 96 miles. There are only five locks, all at Lockport. The cable tow-boat will take five boats through in 30 hours, including any extra delay at locks, which at most will be to the last boat of the tow, 30 minutes. Here is a gain of 35 hours in only 96 miles of the canal.

The Belgian system is as readily used by the present canal boat as animal power. The steering gear must be altered to suit the increased speed, at an expense of $20 and delay of 30 minutes. No trouble is experienced in passing canal boats.

No profits have been made with the two boats now owned by the company. The daily receipts have sometimes exceeded the daily expenses. Only such canal boats employed the cable tow-boats on the very short portion of the canal operated, as could do so with very great saving to their horses. But, when a single line of cable between Buffalo and Rochester can be operated with the necessary number of cable tow-boats, the company is promised the patronage of the owners of the present canal boats now using animal power. The profits must then be large, though the receipts be only what animal power now costs.

The very profitable results of cable towing in Europe is bringing it into more general use there. In the London newspaper, "Engineering," of June 19th, 1874, will be found a drawing and description of the "Leitha," working on the river Danube. A company at Cologne is working on the Rhine a distance of 250 miles, with a capital of 1,200,000 thalers.

The government of Belgium altered its canals at great expense, that this cable system of towing might be worked at greatest advantage, and after obtaining statistics of its very profitable operation before the canals were adapted to it. Other instances of successful operation in Europe can be given.

Never before has the subject of steam on the canals assumed such great importance to the city and State of New York. The general stagnation of trade and the unusually severe competition of railways, have caused almost disastrous results to the individuals, or companies, doing the freighting business upon the Erie canal by means of animal power. The canal, during the past season, has been in remarkably good condition, as regards abundance and depth of water, and reduced power of current. The future of the business upon the canals looks very discouraging, as animal power is the sole reliance at present, and must continue to be, until some form of steam can be successfully and universally applied. Eminent railway officials prophesy the growing of grass in the canals, and this will be the case should there be a succession of unprofitable seasons like that just closed.

What has been done toward using steam on the canals?

For years, efforts have been made to accomplish this, and all of the usual forms of navigating water by steam, using the propeller or paddle, have been tried and abandoned. While admitting the enormous profit attending success, almost all have become skeptical upon the subject, and conclude that animal power, with enlarged locks and increased dimensions of canal, causing enormous outlay of money by the State, together with the abolition of tolls, to be the only remedies. The abolition of tolls — the State resorting to taxation for the maintenance of the canals — would be an immense help to the business.

The State, recognizing the necessity of applying steam to the canals, offered a prize of $100,000 for a successful means of doing this. Proper and rigid provisions, demanded by the experience gained in ascertaining the wants of the business on the canal, were incorporated in the law. One system, the Belgian, was excluded from competition under the law, an amendment being added for the express purpose. The reasons for doing this were understood to be that it was not new, was the only feasible plan, and did not meet the object of the law, viz.: to stimulate the inventive talent of the people. Many efforts were made to comply with the law at large outlay of means, but so unsuccessful were they, that very important changes in the provisions of the law had to be made, and the law was amended to meet the case. Under this fresh impetus old efforts were revived, and many new inventions created. The great object was, to carry 200 tons of freight in a steam canal boat at double the speed of, and cheaper than animal power. Many official trials were made, but none were successful, in the opinion of the eminent commission, appointed under the law to award the prize, and they so reported to the legislature. *There has been no award under that prize law.* The commission did recommend that a law be passed giving a donation to the two most meritorious competitors. This donation was to be awarded as follows: When one of the competitors had placed seven of his boats fully equipped upon the canal, he was to receive $35,000, and under same conditions, the other competitor was to receive $15,000 for three of his boats. This was the only way the State was to legally give money for steam on the canals. Since then, the two competitors have harmonized their interests, and, thus united, claim the award under the donation law recommended by the honorable commission, who could not award this $50,000 under the original amended prize law.

But although it would seem as if the State prize law had been the means of nearly solving this question, yet among those men best qualified to judge of the practical success of these two boats, by reason of their business as produce merchants, as managers of transportation companies working on the canals, or as possessing great knowledge of machinery, there exists great doubt as to the unqualified success publicly claimed by the owners or inventors of these two boats. Have they really done any thing new? If they have made any profits, how do they compare with those of canal boats using animal power? How much money has each boat made? Have they paid expenses? What repairs have been necessitated by practical working? How do the boats rate upon the underwriters' books, and compare with other steam canal boats?

During the past season, a produce firm made a contract for a steam canal boat, to be built under rigid specifications, like those in the State prize law, as to power, carrying capacity, speed, and least expense, the pay for the boat to be forfeited if it failed to meet the provisions of the contract. This boat was rejected. A member of this firm is probably the only merchant belonging to the New York Produce Exchange, who, from great interest in the question of steam on the canals, went on one of the boats from New York to Buffalo and back, that stood best in the estimation of the commissioners of the prize law. It is claimed that the boat his firm refused to pay for, on account of its complete failure, had better machinery than the best boats competing for the State prize.

The seriousness of the subject increases as success approaches. And should the present prize boats fail, a general abandonment of the subject would inevitably follow, as they are the best created by the great stimulus of the $100,000 prize.

But it may be that the solution of this question will come from a rigid investigation of the merits of that system excluded by amendment from the provisions of the prize law. The engineer of the prize commission has made a most favorable report of this system, and, after liberally allowing for the few unfavorable features suggested by his examination of its operations on the canal between Buffalo and Lockport, comes to the conclusion "that the cost of movement proper (by this system), between Buffalo and New York, as compared with that by the present horse boat, is *thirty-six per cent less*," and better by eight to ten per cent than the two steam canal boats he especially favors. His qualifying remarks at the end of the report are not discouraging when the exceedingly exhaustive nature of the report is considered, covering fully all objections that suggested themselves to his able judgment while preparing it. It is said by competent and unprejudiced judges that it is the cheapest known form of applying steam power to shallow water, and the results, as they are shown in the engineer's report to the prize commission, seems to justify this.

A question of the greatest importance is, how to utilize the 5,000 canal boats, now doing the enormous business of the Erie canal, when steam is substituted for animal power. The owners of those boats, representing an investment of nearly $20,000,000 of money, are unable, as a rule, to apply steam machinery to them, even was an approved form known of at the present time, for the additional cost would be equal to the present investment. These owners grant the necessity of some power other than animal, and will gladly adopt it if practically and economically offered. This must at least be something that is as cheap as horse power, and, if possible, give the great benefits coming from increased speed. They, and all important judges of the wants of the canals and its business, see no relief in any, even the best, of the steam canal boats created by the prize law. The State commission confirm this by their report to the legislature, and their inability to award the State prize.

The efforts of the promoters of these new steam canal boats are entirely devoted to placing on the canal new boats of peculiar construction of hull and machinery, rather than applying machinery to the present horse canal boats, upon which the enormous trade now done annually upon the canals, solely depends.

But the most serious trouble arises from the almost ruinous rates of freight paid owners of canal boats during the past season, and if continued in future seasons, must result in the stoppage of all business on the canals now using animal power. It will be seen that no form of steam canal boat, restricting the application of its power to the 250 tons of cargo it carries, can remedy this present most serious aspect of canal transportation. It cannot be done as cheaply as animal power, though double speed be uniformly obtained. The solution can only come through some application of steam that will, at the same cost as animal power, move more tons. Large propellers cannot profitably be used in narrow inland water channels like canals — cannot be used at all until the Erie canal is enlarged. If the present steam canal boats, with the same cost, could carry 500 tons, then they would supersede animal power.

The aim of all efforts to introduce steam on the canals, is to cheapen transportation, and increase the tonnage annually moved between the West and the Atlantic. The best means of transportation is by the lakes, Erie canal, and Hudson river. No other plan is as capacious, feasible and cheap, and the present commercial supremacy of New York city cannot pass to other seaboard cities, if the present carrying capacity of the Erie canal can be developed. Although an average of 6,000,000 of tons of freight are transported on the canal every season, yet its present capacity, based upon double locks and a lockage of four minutes, is estimated by the State engineer to be over 18,000,000 of tons. On the Delaware and Hudson canal, modern drop gates are used at the locks, and lockages are made in two minutes. This improvement, applied to the Erie canal, would make its capacity 36,000,000 of tons, which is equal to any demands of trade. The solution of the question of cheap transportation rests as much upon the increased amount of freight transported, as upon increased speed obtained. If double the present tonnage is transported at present speed and cost of animal power, a great gain results. Increased tonnage diminishes cost of transportation. For instance, the tolls on double the present tonnage could be one-half what they now are, and the State receive the same amount of revenue. This would reduce the freight one and one-half cents on a bushel of wheat. Increased speed increases this great gain, according to its relation to the present speed by animal power, by which 6,000,000 of tons are now moved in a season. The perfect solution of the question of cheap transportation is reached when the extreme capacity of the Erie canal is utilized, and the means which nearest accomplishes this is the best, and regulates the business of the canal by simple laws of trade. What, then, is the best, cheapest, and quickest way to develop this enormous capacity of the Erie canal? Improved gates, enlarged locks or dimensions of canal, while increasing the capacity, only increase the present difficulties. Some new means of transporting freight must be found. The best steam canal boats are inadequate to do this. The increased speed claimed for them would be neutralized, when the 5,000 canal boats have had steam applied to them, on account of the consequent increased risks of collision. A direct railroad from the west to the Atlantic, without grades, constructed in the most substantial manner, transporting freight at the most economical rate of speed, cannot cheapen transportation to the extent afforded by the lakes and Erie canal. On the best managed railroads, between the west and seaboard, freight is not now transported at a less cost to the railroad company than one cent per ton a mile. Some years hence, it is claimed, the cost will be reduced as low as six-tenths of a cent a ton a mile, at a speed not to exceed six miles the hour. This makes the freight on a ton of wheat from Chicago to New York, cost about $5.50. When the present capacity of the Erie canal is utilized, a ton of wheat can be taken by lakes and canal from Chicago to New York at about $4.00, and pay a profit. Increased speed and power upon the Erie canal, at a cost that admits of its substitution for animal power, will meet all demands of cheap transportation. The Belgian system does this, as the foregoing facts prove, and as its application to the Erie canal approaches perfection, the minimum cost of transportation will be reached. The speed, with 2,500 tons in tow, may exceed six miles an hour; the power is limited only to the size of the cable and capacity of engine. Any new motor can be adapted, but no improvement or invention other than this, develops such positive connection and complete utilization of power between the boat moved and the water that floats it.

What, then, prevents the realization of these great advantages to State, city and individual from cheap transportation? Only the money — not exceeding $300,000 — and in a way that combines simplicity, safety and great profit. Compare this amount with any scheme publicly presented. The canals are taken as they are, saving proposed enlargement at immense cost. No money or legislation is wanted from the State. The company's charter is ample for present or future wants. The system is strongly supported by all canal men, and the most imperative demands are made by them for the equipment of the canal by the opening of navigation in the spring. Financially, it must be a success. Any form of steam that is substituted for animal power possesses a virtual lease of the canal. The business awaiting is determined by State statistics. The receipts, based upon a charge for towing that is the same as present cost of animal power, can be accurately estimated. The boatmen promise to pay such charge, they receiving the benefit of double speed at least, which doubles the season's trips and largely increases their income. The actual expenses are known, and the number of cable tow-boats required to tow the canal boats, now the sole reliance of the vast business coming to and greatly benefiting the merchants and real estate owners of the city of New York.

APPENDIX.

Copy of the law authorizing the employment of this system of towage upon the canals of the State of New York.

CHAPTER 576, LAWS OF 1870.

AN ACT to provide for the introduction of the European system of steam towage upon the canals of this State.

PASSED May 2, 1870; three-fifths being present.

The People of the State of New York, represented in Senate and Assembly, do enact as follows:

SECTION 1. Permission is hereby granted to ADDISON M. FARWELL, of Watertown, New York, his associates and successors, who may organize a corporation under the act entitled "An act to authorize the formation of corporations for manufacturing, mining, mechanical and chemical purposes," passed February seventeen, eighteen hundred and forty-eight, and any act or acts amendatory thereof, to introduce upon the canals of this State the "European system" of steam towing.

§ 2. The said FARWELL, his associates and successors, who shall organize as provided in previous section, are hereby authorized and empowered to tow boats, floats and cargoes on the canals of this State, for hire, and for that purpose may purchase and construct, or cause to be constructed, the necessary appliances for carrying on the business of canal towing, under the said European method, and shall have the exclusive right and privilege, during the term for which said corporation may be organized, to submerge or place one or more chains or cables on the bottom of the canals of this State, and attach the same thereto in such manner as will not interfere with navigation; and shall have the exclusive right to use such submerged chains and cables, designated and known as the European system, in the prosecution of the peculiar method of towing thereby. And whenever and wherever it may be necessary so to do, the said FARWELL, his associates and successors, or corporation aforesaid, are hereby authorized and empowered to own and employ other motive power in connection with said chain or cable process, provided the same shall not interfere with navigation. Nothing, however, in this section contained shall be construed as excluding other parties from the right or privilege of propelling or towing themselves or others by the agency of steamboats, propellers, elevated railway or animal power, but simply to vest in the said FARWELL, his associates and successors, or corporation organized as aforesaid, the exclusive right to lay and use chains or cables in the prosecution of the European system of towing thereby.

§ 3. Any person who shall meddle with or disturb the chains or cables, authorized to be laid under this act, with intent to injure the same, or in any manner to embarrass the operation thereof, or any person who shall willfully obstruct or interfere with boats rightfully using said chains or cables, or towed thereby, shall be deemed guilty of a misdemeanor, punishable by fine or imprisonment, the fine not to exceed $200, and imprisonment not to exceed three months. And any person who shall willfully injure the chains or cables as aforesaid, or by other improper conduct shall detain the boats rightfully using said chains or cables, or being towed thereby, shall be liable to the parties aggrieved for all damages occasioned by said injury or detention.

§ 4. The tugs, with machinery connected therewith, employed by said FARWELL, his associates and successors, or corporation aforesaid, in the prosecution of towing, together with the fuel necessary to the voyage, carried thereon, shall be exempt from the payment of tolls.

§ 5. In case said FARWELL, his associates and successors, or corporation aforesaid, shall neglect or fail to introduce said system of towing on the Erie canal within eighteen months after the passage of this act, all rights and privileges herein granted shall cease.

§ 6. Nothing herein contained shall be construed to exclude the system of towage hereby authorized from the supervision and control of the Canal Board, but the same shall be subject to all the rules and regulations from time to time established by the Canal Board for the navigation of the canals.

§ 7. The Legislature may at any time alter, modify or repeal this act.

§ 8. This act shall take effect immediately.

STATE OF NEW YORK,
Office of Secretary of State. } *ss:*

I have compared the preceding with the original law on file in this office, and do hereby certify that the same is a correct transcript therefrom and of the whole of said original law.

HOMER A. NELSON,
Secretary of State.

CHAPTER 93, LAWS OF 1872.

AN ACT to confer additional powers upon the New York Steam Cable Towing Company, a corporation organized pursuant to the requirements of chapter five hundred and seventy-six of the Laws of eighteen hundred and seventy, and to authorize said company to issue the preferred stock and bonds thereof.

PASSED March 8, 1872; three-fifths being present.

The People of the State of New York, represented in Senate and Assembly, do enact as follows:

SECTION 1. In addition to the powers and privileges conferred upon ADDISON M. FARWELL, his associates and successors, by act chapter five hundred and seventy-six of the laws of one thousand eight hundred and seventy, entitled "An act to provide for the introduction of the European system of steam towage upon the canals of this State;" the New York Steam Cable Towing Company, a corporation duly organized in conformity with the provisions of "An act to authorize the formation of corporations for manufacturing, mining, mechanical and chemical purposes," and the several acts amendatory thereof, as provided in the aforesaid act first mentioned, shall have power to build, purchase, import, own, charter, equip and furnish all such boats, tugs, towers, chains, cables and other machinery and apparatus as may be necessary to apply and operate the said European system in the towage and propulsion of boats and floats upon the canals of this State, subject to the approval, in all cases, of the Canal Board. The New York Steam Cable Towing Company may also purchase, own, hire, lease and convey such real and personal property as may be necessary in the execution of the business contemplated in its charter and certificate of incorporation.

§ 2. Whenever the written assent of the stockholders owning at least two-thirds of the capital stock of the company shall have been obtained and filed, as hereinafter provided, the trustees of said company may, for the purpose of procuring the means necessary for equipping the canals with the system of steam cable towage, issue the preferred stock of the company, and make and issue the bonds of said company, and secure the same by mortgage of the franchises of said company, and also of all or any part of its real and personal estate; and every such mortgage shall, to all intents and purposes, be as valid as if executed by an individual owning such real and personal estate. Such assent shall be filed, and every such mortgage shall be recorded in the office of the clerk of the county where the principal office company is located. And it is hereby declared that such filing and recording shall be a sufficient compliance with the laws on this subject, except as to mortgages upon the real estate of said company, which shall be recorded as now provided by law.

§ 3. This act shall take effect immediately.

STATE OF NEW YORK, }
Office of Secretary of State. } *ss.:*

I have compared the preceding with the original law on file in this office, and do hereby certify that the same is a correct transcript therefrom, and of the whole of said original law.

[L. S.] Given under my hand and seal of office, at the city of Albany, this eighth day of March, in the year one thousand eight hundred and seventy-two.

G. HILTON SCRIBNER,
Secretary of State.

COPY OF BOND.

No. ...... UNITED STATES OF AMERICA. STATE OF NEW YORK. **$1,000.**

Six per cent Gold, Sinking Fund and Participating Bond of

THE NEW YORK STEAM CABLE TOWING COMPANY,

Incorporated November 1, 1871. SECURED BY FIRST MORTGAGE Whole issue, **$800,000.**

Upon its Franchises and Property pertaining to the Buffalo and Rochester Division of the Erie Canal.

The New York Steam Cable Towing Company, a corporation formed and existing under the general and special laws of the State of New York, is indebted to   in the sum of One Thousand Dollars, which the said company promises to pay in gold coin to the registered owner hereof, on the first day of April, in the year one thousand eight hundred and eighty-three, together with interest thereon from and after the date hereof, at the rate of six per centum per annum, payable semi-annually, in gold coin, at the banking house of The New York Guaranty and Indemnity Company, in the City of New York, on the first day of April and October in each year.

If default shall be made in the payment of any interest of this bond, and if default shall continue for the period of six months, and if such interest shall be afterward demanded at the place where the same is payable, then, on any failure to pay such interest so demanded, the whole principal of this bond, and of all other bonds of the same series which shall have been issued, and shall then be outstanding, shall thereupon be and become forthwith due and payable, any thing herein contained to the contrary thereof notwithstanding.

This bond is one of a series of eight hundred bonds of the same tenor and date, and numbered consecutively from one to eight hundred, both inclusive, for the sum of one thousand dollars each, and amounting, in the aggregate, to eight hundred thousand dollars. The payment of the principal and interest of all of said bonds is alike, and equally secured by a mortgage or deed of trust, bearing even date herewith, made, executed, and delivered by this company to the said The New York Guaranty and Indemnity Company, upon all the real and personal estate, boats, towing cables, franchises, business, profits and property of this company, acquired or to be hereafter acquired, being in the use or possession, or to come into the use or possession of this company, or in any wise appertaining to its business of Cable Towing by steam upon the two levels of the Erie canal, from Buffalo to Lockport, and from Lockport to Rochester, in the State of New York, as particularly expressed in said mortgage.

This bond is entitled to the benefit of a Sinking Fund of ten per centum of the net earnings of the company, to be deposited annually, on the first day of April, with the trustee, as provided in and by said mortgage. And the owner of this bond is also entitled, on the first day of every April hereafter, to a *pro rata* participation in all such net earnings of this company as shall be realized from its business upon the two levels aforesaid, during the year ending the thirty-first day of the previous December, after deducting therefrom interest on this issue of its bonds and ten per centum for the sinking fund, such participation to be equal to one-half of said net earnings to the extent and amount of six per centum per annum on the amount of the principal of this bond. And this company hereby binds itself to pay such additional six per centum, or so much thereof as shall be realized as aforesaid, in gold coin, at the banking house of The New York Guaranty and Indemnity Company, on the first day of every April hereafter, until this bond is paid.

This bond shall pass only by assignment indorsed hereon, and by transfer on the books of the company, in the city of New York, which transfer books the company may close during the fifteen days next preceding the date herein fixed for the payment of interest.

In Witness Whereof, the said The New York Steam Cable Towing Company has caused its corporate seal to be hereunto affixed, and these presents to be subscribed by its President, and attested by its Secretary, and to certify that the said trustee is possessed of the said mortgage, and that this bond is one of the said eight hundred bonds, secured thereby, the said The New York Guaranty and Indemnity Company, as trustee, has, by its President, countersigned this [illegible] the first day of April, in the year of our Lord, one thousand eight hundred and seventy-three.

[L. S.] *President.*

Secretary.

The New York Guaranty and Indemnity Company,

Trustee.

President.

www.ingramcontent.com/pod-product-compliance
Lightning Source LLC
LaVergne TN
LVHW011147110826
845150LV00008B/2555
9781418192440